WNBA Hot Ticket

DALLAS WINGS

JOSH ANDERSON

Lerner Publications ◆ Minneapolis

The stats and information in this book are accurate through July 2024.

Lerner Publications Company
An imprint of Lerner Publishing Group, Inc.
241 First Avenue North
Minneapolis, MN 55401 USA

For reading levels and more information, look up this title at www.lernerbooks.com.

Main body text set in Aptifer Slab LT Pro / Typeface provided by Linotype AG

Library of Congress Cataloging-in-Publication Data

Names: Anderson, Josh, author.
Title: Dallas Wings / Josh Anderson.
Description: Minneapolis, MN : Lerner Publications, 2025. | Series: WNBA hot ticket (Lerner sports) | Includes bibliographical references and index. | Audience: Ages 7–11 | Audience: Grades 2–3 | Summary: "In 2010, the WNBA's Detroit Shock moved to Tulsa, Oklahoma. Seven years later, they moved again and became the Dallas Wings. Explore the team's history, great players, and biggest wins"—Provided by publisher.
Identifiers: LCCN 2024030327 (print) | LCCN 2024030328 (ebook) | ISBN 9798765669747 (library binding) | ISBN 9798765669860 (paperback) | ISBN 9798765669884 (epub)
Subjects: LCSH: Dallas Wings (Basketball team)—Juvenile literature. | Women's National Basketball Association—Juvenile literature. | Women basketball players—United States—Juvenile literature.
Classification: LCC GV885.52.D35 A53 2025 (print) | LCC GV885.52.D35 (ebook) | DDC 796.323/64097642812—dc23/eng/20240702

LC record available at https://lccn.loc.gov/2024030327
LC ebook record available at https://lccn.loc.gov/2024030328

Manufactured in the United States of America
1 - CG - 12/15/24

TABLE OF CONTENTS

Deanna Nolan averaged 15.5 points and 2.6 assists per game during the 2003 WNBA playoffs.

A HEROIC THREE-POINTER

FACTS AT A GLANCE

- The **DETROIT SHOCK** won three titles in six seasons from 2003 to 2008.
- The team moved to Tulsa, Oklahoma, in 2010 and played as the **TULSA SHOCK**. In 2016, they moved to Dallas, Texas, and became the Dallas Wings.
- In 2018, **LIZ CAMBAGE** scored 53 points for the Wings. She set an all-time Women's National Basketball Association (WNBA) record for most points in a game.
- The **WINGS** made the playoffs three seasons in a row from 2021 to 2023.

The Dallas Wings have played their home games in three different cities. In 2003, they were called the Detroit Shock and played home games in Detroit, Michigan. That season, the Shock made it all the way to the WNBA Finals.

In Game 2 of the Finals, the Shock's Deanna Nolan hit two free throws in the closing seconds. The Shock won the game and tied the series with the Los Angeles Sparks. Two nights later, the winner of Game 3 would become WNBA champions. The Shock had never won the championship.

In Game 3, Detroit built up an early lead. But by halftime, the Sparks had nearly caught up to them. With under a minute left in the game, Los Angeles led 75–72. Sparks star Lisa Leslie missed a short jump shot. Shock center Ruth Riley grabbed the rebound for Detroit and headed up the court.

Swin Cash held the ball for Detroit outside the three-point line, eyeing the Sparks defense. She tossed a pass to Shock guard Elaine Powell a few feet behind the free-throw line. Powell dribbled to her left and then fired a pass to Nolan, the Game 2 hero.

Nolan was standing in the corner behind the three-point line. Before a Sparks defender could get there to defend her, Nolan rose up and shot a three-pointer. The ball swished through the net as Nolan jumped in excitement. She hit four free throws in the final minute, and the Shock won the game 83–78.

Shock players celebrate their 2003 WNBA title.

Ruth Riley (*right*) played for five teams during her 13-year WNBA career. She won two titles with the Shock.

The Shock won the 2003 WNBA championship and two more titles in the five years that followed. But since then, the team has been searching for another big win. They became the Dallas Wings in 2016. When the Wings made the playoffs in 2023, it was the first time in almost 15 years that the team had made the playoffs three seasons in a row. With top stars Satou Sabally and Arike Ogunbowale leading the way, Dallas may soon reach the Finals again.

After coaching the Shock for three seasons from 1998 to 2000, Nancy Lieberman returned to the team for one game as a player in 2008. At 50, she set the record as the oldest WNBA player in history.

CHAPTER 1

FROM SHOCK TO WINGS

In 1997, the WNBA began with eight teams. The Detroit Shock started play the following year as an expansion team. The team's name honored Detroit's history in the auto industry. Shock absorbers, or shocks, are parts that help cars drive more smoothly.

With women's basketball legend Nancy Lieberman coaching the team, the Shock had a winning record in their first year. They made the playoffs in the team's second season. In 2002, the Shock hired Detroit legend Bill Laimbeer as their coach. Laimbeer had won two National Basketball Association (NBA) championships as a player for the Detroit Pistons.

Bill Laimbeer (*right*) coached three different teams during his 17 seasons in the WNBA.

Laimbeer led the Shock to WNBA titles in 2003, 2006, and 2008. After making the playoffs under new coach Rick Mahorn in 2009, the WNBA announced that the Shock would leave Detroit for Tulsa. The team needed to earn more money to stay in business. They thought moving to Tulsa would help.

The Tulsa Shock didn't have much success. They finished last or next-to-last in the Western Conference in five of their six seasons. Ahead of the 2016 season, the team announced their move to Dallas. The move came with a new name—the Dallas Wings. The team's colors changed from black, red, and gold, to blue, lime green, and white.

While the team hasn't matched their past success since moving to Dallas, there have been many highlights. The Wings have made the playoffs five times since arriving in Texas. In 2018, Liz Cambage scored

Liz Cambage (*right*) passes to a teammate around a New York Liberty guard during a 2018 game.

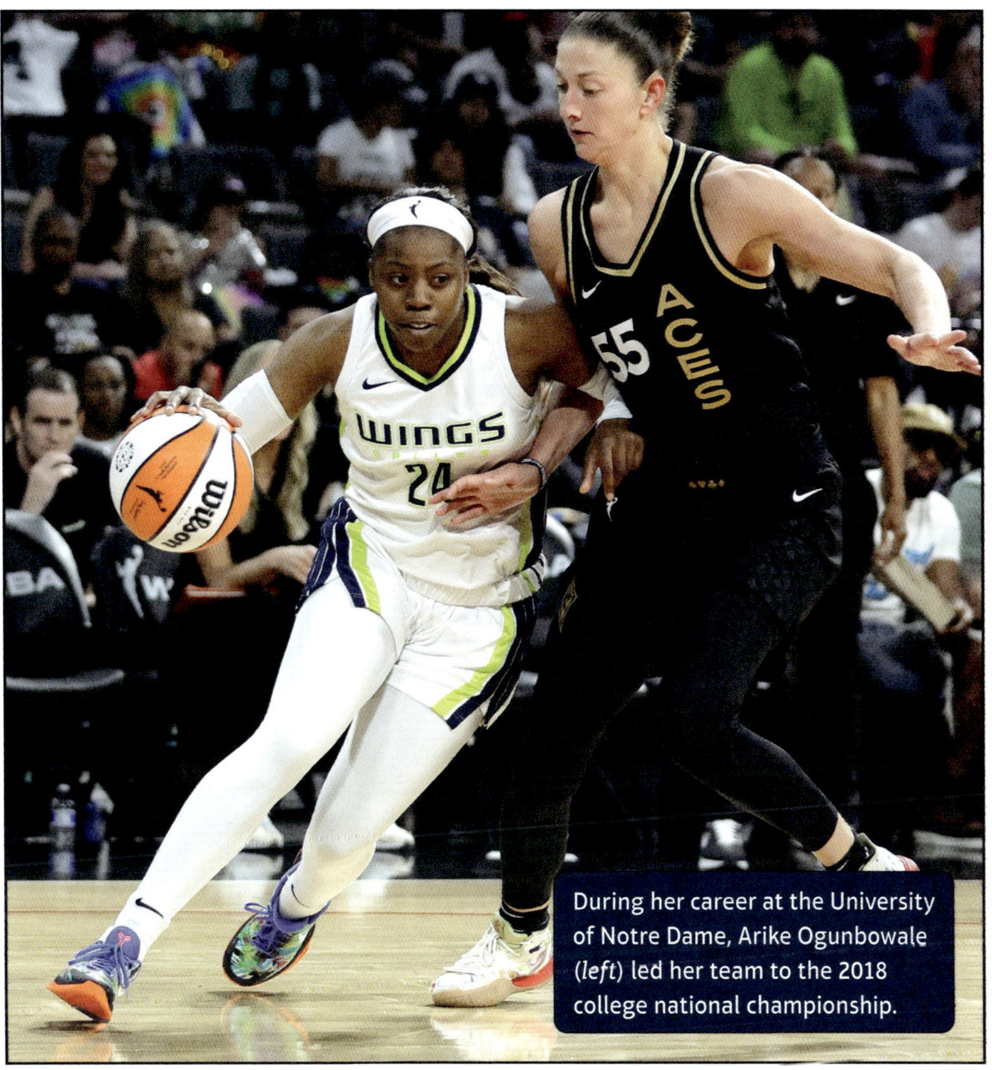

During her career at the University of Notre Dame, Arike Ogunbowale (*left*) led her team to the 2018 college national championship.

53 points against the New York Liberty. She set a record for the most points in a game in league history.

In 2019, the Wings picked guard Arike Ogunbowale in the first round of the WNBA Draft. In 2020, the team chose forward Satou Sabally. The two young stars have each been All-WNBA First Team players early in their careers.

HOOPS SCOOP

The Wings' top pick in the 2023 WNBA Draft was forward Maddy Siegrist from Villanova University.

Maddy Siegrist (*right*) was the third overall pick in the 2023 WNBA Draft.

In 2023, the Wings had their first winning season in Dallas. The Wings also won their first playoff series since 2009. Coach Latricia Trammell was hired in 2023 and hopes to build on the success of her first season. She wants to help the Wings build a winning tradition in Dallas.

COMMUNITY FOUNDATION

The Dallas Wings Community Foundation works hard to make a positive impact on the people of Dallas. The foundation focuses on women and girls, social justice, youth sports, health and wellness, and education. One way the Wings help give money to the community is through a raffle at every home game. Fans donate money, and then a raffle winner is drawn. The winner gets half of the money, while the other half helps people in the community.

The Wings and other WNBA teams work hard off the court to promote women's health.

HOOPS SCOOP

The Shock sent four players to the WNBA All-Star Game in 2005: Swin Cash, Cheryl Ford, Deanna Nolan, and Ruth Riley.

Deanna Nolan dribbles to the basket during Game 3 of the 2008 WNBA Finals.

CHAPTER 2

ALL-TIME GREATS

The years 2003 to 2008 were the best seasons for the Detroit Shock. During that time, the team won three WNBA titles and had three of the best players in the league. One of them was Deanna Nolan. A four-time All-Star, Nolan is the team's all-time leader in points, assists, and steals. She won the WNBA Finals Most Valuable Player (MVP) award in 2006.

Nolan and her teammate, forward Cheryl Ford, both played their entire WNBA careers for the Shock. Like Nolan, Ford was a WNBA All-Star four times. Ford is the Wings' all-time leader in rebounds. She was chosen as the 2003 WNBA Rookie of the Year, and she was MVP of the WNBA All-Star Game in 2007.

Cheryl Ford played all seven of her WNBA seasons with the Detroit Shock.

Swin Cash played the first 6 of her 15 WNBA seasons for the Shock. Cash was chosen as an All-Star twice during her time in Detroit. She's 1 of only 13 players in history to win an Olympic gold medal, a college national championship, an International Basketball Federation World Cup gold medal, and a WNBA title.

Swin Cash's 1,397 made free throws rank 10th all-time in the WNBA. Her 2,521 rebounds rank 14th.

The Shock's coach for all three of their WNBA titles was Bill Laimbeer. Laimbeer was known for his tough play during his NBA career. He tried to get his team to play hard defense like his championship Pistons teams did. After leaving the Shock, Laimbeer coached the New York Liberty and Las Vegas Aces.

Guard Skylar Diggins-Smith played for the Shock during their last three seasons in Tulsa. She moved with the team to Dallas where she played three more seasons. Diggins-Smith was a four-time All-Star during her time with the team. She helped lead them to the playoffs three times and led the team in scoring during three different seasons.

Skylar Diggins-Smith (*right*) dribbles past a Connecticut Sun defender during a 2014 game.

The Wings chose forward Satou Sabally with the second overall pick in the 2020 WNBA Draft. Sabally made an impact in her first season, averaging 13.9 points and 7.8 rebounds per game. She was first chosen as an All-Star during the 2021 season. Then, in 2023, Sabally became one of the best players in the WNBA when she averaged 18.6 points, 8.1 rebounds, 4.4 assists, and 1.8 steals. She won the 2023 Most Improved Player award and was a member of the All-WNBA First Team.

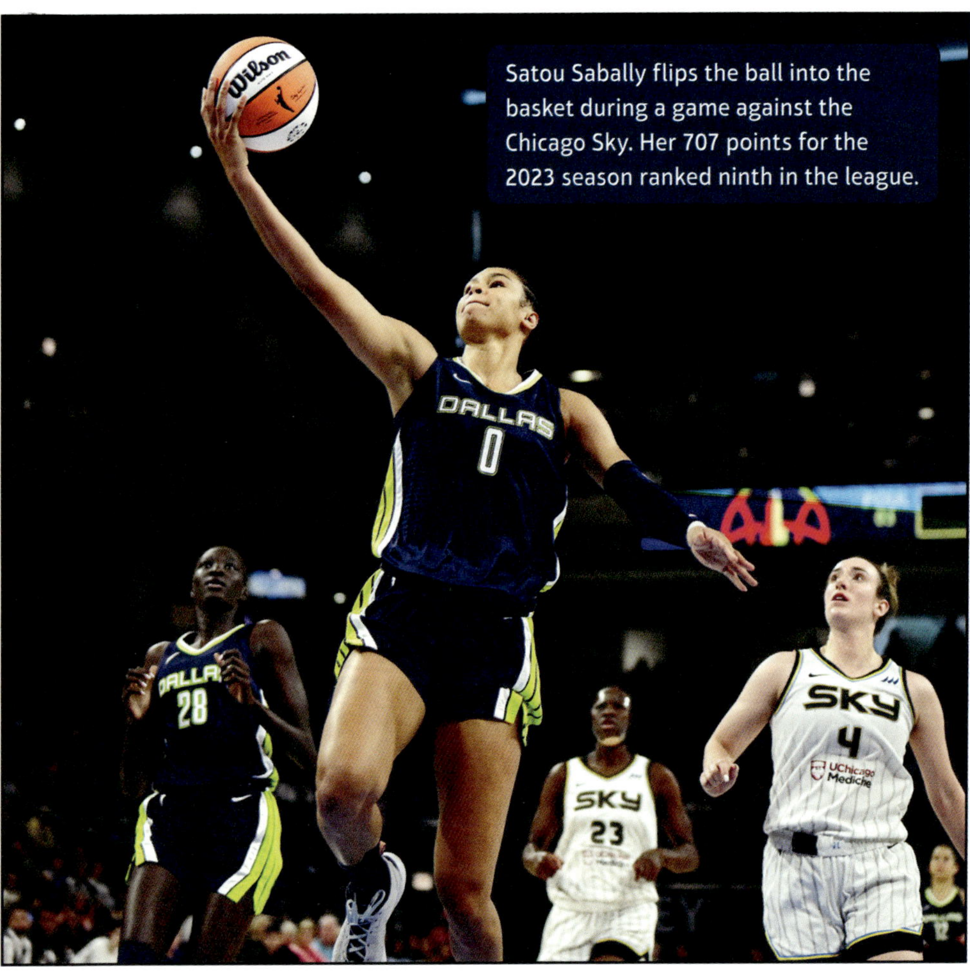

Satou Sabally flips the ball into the basket during a game against the Chicago Sky. Her 707 points for the 2023 season ranked ninth in the league.

Arike Ogunbowale averaged a career-high 22.8 points per game during her second season with the Wings.

Guard Arike Ogunbowale joined the Wings as the team's top pick in the 2019 WNBA Draft. She led the league in scoring in 2020 and was part of the All-WNBA First Team. A four-time All-Star, Ogunbowale put on a great show at the 2021 WNBA All-Star Game. She played for a team of WNBA All-Stars competing against the US Olympic Women's Basketball Team. Ogunbowale scored 26 points and won the game's MVP award, leading the WNBA All-Stars to victory.

Kayla Thornton (*left*) gets the rebound after a missed shot from the Atlanta Dream's Monique Billings in 2021.

CHAPTER 3

AMAZING MOMENTS

By 2023, it had been 14 seasons since the Dallas Wings had won a playoff series. The team had only won a single playoff game since 2009. Behind new coach Latricia Trammell, the Wings were determined to win Game 1 of their 2023 first-round series against the Atlanta Dream. A win would put them on a path to reach the next round of the WNBA playoffs.

The game's first half was a roller coaster for the Wings. Atlanta built a 36–21 lead in the first quarter. Dallas roared back to tie the game before halftime. With about seven minutes left in the game, Atlanta's Aari McDonald hit a layup to put the Dream up 76–73.

Latricia Trammell spent 23 years as a high school and college coach before joining the WNBA in 2017.

Dallas had been the better team all season. Arike Ogunbowale, Satou Sabally, and Natasha Howard were three of the best players in the WNBA. The Wings stars would need to take over if they were going to avoid losing Game 1.

Less than a minute later, Sabally hit a three-pointer to tie the game 76–76. With about five minutes remaining, Sabally drove to the hoop for a basket, putting Dallas up 80–76. After Atlanta answered with a basket of their own, the Wings' Teaira McCowan fired a pass to Ogunbowale. Ogunbowale sank a jump shot to put the Wings back up by four.

Satou Sabally scored 79 points and grabbed 26 rebounds during the 2023 playoffs.

Natasha Howard shoots a three-pointer to give the Wings a five-point lead over the Atlanta Dream during Game 1 of the 2023 playoffs.

Moments later, Ogunbowale threw a pass to Howard. Howard hit a three-pointer with just under four minutes remaining and put the Wings up 85–80. Dallas built on their lead from there, finishing with a 94–82 victory. The Wings would go on to win the series against the Dream before losing in the next round to the Las Vegas Aces.

HOOPS SCOOP

Arike Ogunbowale has finished in the top five in scoring average every season of her WNBA career.

Arike Ogunbowale (*left*) dribbles around Layshia Clarendon of the Los Angeles Sparks during a 2024 game.

Another incredible moment in team history took place a few years earlier in June 2018. That night, Liz Cambage took aim at the WNBA's single-game scoring record. Coming into the game, the most points ever scored in a WNBA contest was 51. That was done by the Tulsa Shock's Riquna Williams in 2013.

Cambage had an incredible night against the New York Liberty. She was one point behind Williams's record as time wound down. With 45 seconds left in the game and the Wings up by 16 points, Cambage took a pass at the top of the three-point line. She fired the ball toward the hoop, and it fell through the net. The basket gave Cambage 53 points and set a new record for the league. Cambage's amazing point total was tied in 2023 by A'ja Wilson of the Las Vegas Aces.

Liz Cambage (*left*) was the leading scorer for her home country of Australia during the 2016 Olympics.

Arike Ogunbowale breaks through two Phoenix Mercury defenders to score during a 2024 game.

CHAPTER 4

WAITING IN THE WINGS

Few teams in the WNBA can claim a period of success as great as the Detroit Shock's from 2003 to 2008. But the years since then have been hard for fans of the team. Two moves and too few winning seasons have resulted in hard times for the Wings. But the team has found a home in Dallas, and building a winning tradition on the court and winning in the playoffs are the next steps.

The Wings celebrate a 2024 win over the Seattle Storm.

After two straight first-round playoff losses, the Wings hired Latricia Trammell ahead of the 2023 season. Trammell knows defense. She focused largely on defense as a Los Angeles Sparks assistant coach from 2019 to 2022. She helped four Sparks players earn a spot on the league's All-Defensive Team. Wings fans hope Trammell can bring a strong defense to a team that already has three top scorers in Howard, Sabally, and Ogunbowale.

Ogunbowale showed even more progress in 2024. She became one of the best scorers in the WNBA. Her growth and Howard and Sabally's amazing skills could go a long way toward bringing a title to Dallas.

With rising stars such as Arike Ogunbowale (*left*) and Satou Sabally (*right*) on the team, the Wings have what it takes to make the playoffs every season.

Natasha Howard leaps past two Los Angeles Sparks defenders and shoots the ball during a 2024 game.

GLOSSARY

All-WNBA First Team: a team that honors the best players in the WNBA each season

assist: a pass that leads directly to a basket

draft: when teams take turns choosing new players

expansion team: a team added to an existing sports league

layup: a shot in basketball made from near the basket, usually by playing the ball off the backboard

playoffs: games held after the season to determine each year's champion

rebound: grabbing and controlling the ball after a missed shot

rookie: a first-year player

steal: when a basketball player takes the ball from an opposing player

title: championship

WNBA Finals: the last series of the season to determine the league champion

LEARN MORE

Berglund, Bruce. *Basketball GOATs: The Greatest Athletes of All Time*. North Mankato, MN: Capstone Press, 2022.

Dallas Wings
https://wings.wnba.com/

Doeden, Matt. Basketball's *Biggest Rivalries*. North Mankato, MN: Capstone Press, 2024.

Leed, Percy. *Pro Basketball by the Numbers*. Minneapolis: Lerner Publications, 2025.

Whiting, Jim. *The Story of the Dallas Wings*. Mankato, MN: Creative Education and Creative Paperbacks, 2024.

WNBA
https://www.wnba.com/

INDEX

PHOTO ACKNOWLEDGMENTS

Image credits: Image credits: Tom Pidgeon/Getty Images Sport/Getty Images, p.4; Tom Pidgeon/Getty Images Sport/Getty Images, p.6; Tom Pidgeon/Getty Images Sport/Getty Images, p.7; Mitchell Layton/Getty Images Sport/Getty Images, p.8; Gregory Shamus/Getty Images Sport/Getty Images, p. 9; Meg Oliphant/Getty Images Sport/Getty Images, p.10; Ethan Miller/Getty Images Sport/Getty Images, p.11; Sarah Stier/Getty Images Sport/Getty Images, p.12; Erica Denhoff/Icon Sportswire/Getty Images, p.13; Domenic Centofanti/Getty Images Sport/Getty Images, p.14; Jed Jacobsohn/Getty Images Sport/Getty Images, p.15; Chris Graythen/Getty Images Sport/Getty Images, p.16; Tim Clayton/Corbis/Getty Images, p.17; Quinn Harris/Getty Images Sport/Getty Images, p.18; Cooper Neill/Getty Images Sport/Getty Images, p.19; Tom Pennington/Getty Images Sport/Getty Images, p.20; Candice Ward/Getty Images Sport/Getty Images, p.21; Maximillian Haupt/picture alliance/Getty Images, p.22; Jevone Moore/Icon Sportswire/Getty Images, p.23; Ronald Martinez/Getty Images Sport/Getty Images, p.24; ANDREJ ISAKOVIC/AFP/Getty Images, p.25; Christian Petersen/Getty Images Sport/Getty Images, p.26; Abbie Parr/Getty Images Sport/Getty Images, p.27; Ethan Miller/Getty Images Sport/Getty Images, p.28; Jevone Moore/Icon Sportswire/Getty Images, p. 29

Cover image: Abbie Parr/Getty Images Sport/Getty Images